Lena the LION

Come on a great adventure with me and learn about my family

TRUE TO LIFE BOOKS

Educating children about endangered animals.

Jan Latta author and wildlife photographer.

Hello! My name is Lena and I am a lion.

I live on the grasslands of Africa
with my family.
We are called a **pride** of lions.

My father has a magnificent **mane** of hair around his head.

My father is bigger than my mother,
and weighs up to 190 kilograms.

My mother is smaller and measures about
2.7 metres from her nose to the tip of her tail.

My mother looks after her new cubs.
They will drink her rich milk for a year.

Then she will teach them how to hunt
and they will start to eat meat.

We have lots of **fun** together.

We play and wrestle for hours. We even try to climb trees!

We always greet each other by rubbing our heads together. Then we **groom** each other.

We keep ourselves very clean. We comb our fur with our rough tongues, just like house cats.

We **hun**t in the cool of the evening.
We crawl along, hidden by the tall grass and bushes.
At the right moment, we charge and pounce.

We keep ourselves very clean. We comb our fur with our rough tongues, just like house cats.

We like to curl up together and **sleep** for most of the day, because it's so hot.

In the afternoon we wake up, have a big stretch, then it is time to go hunting.

We **hun**t in the cool of the evening.
We crawl along, hidden by the tall grass and bushes.
At the right moment, we charge and pounce.

Lions are **carnivores**, which means we eat meat. The males always eat first after a kill, then the females and lastly, the cubs.

In the morning the pride returns home. Look at our full tummies!

See my paw-prints in the dirt?
They are called **pug marks**. I have soft pads on my paws and retractable claws.

Did you know we have spots when
we are young? They fade as we grow older.

If a warthog is hiding under the ground,
we can dig a big hole with our paws and claws.

Oops!

We have very good eyesight,
strong teeth and powerful jaws.

Making a face helps us **smell** other animals.
We wrinkle our nose, lift our head and open our mouth.

We **communicate** by growling and roaring.
Look at our sharp teeth!

My father has the loudest roar of all. You can hear his deep throaty sound over eight kilometres away!

LION FACTS

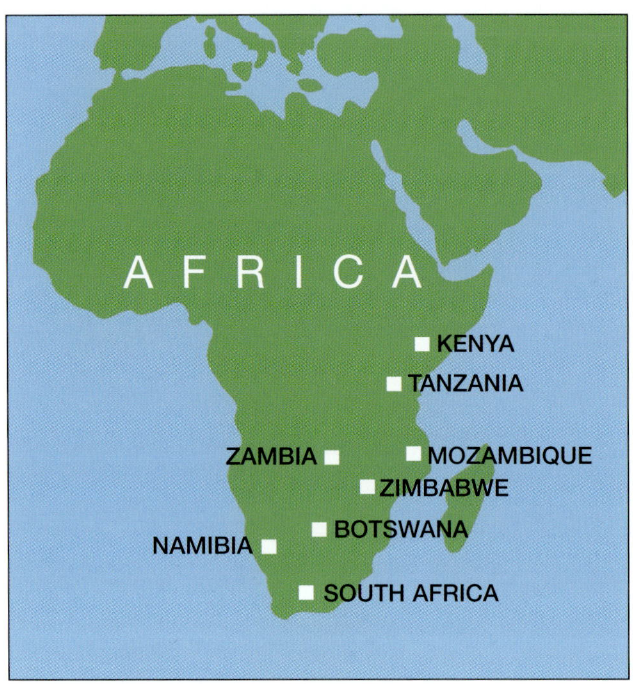

Some of the areas where lions can be found

SCIENTIFIC NAME

Panthera Leo.
Further classified into 7 sub-species: 6 African (1 extinct) and 1 Asiatic.

HABITAT The African lion inhabits grassy plains, open woodlands and scrub country. They generally avoid dense forests.

WEIGHT

Males weigh up to 190 kg.
Females weigh up to 130 kg.

HEIGHT

Average shoulder height:
Male 1.2 metres
Female 90 cm.

LENGTH

Length from nose to tail-tip:
Male 3 metres
Female 2.7 metres.

BIRTH Cubs are born blind and weigh 1.3 kg to 1.8 kg. The fur is often spotted or striped. Cubs are introduced to the pride when they are 4 to 6 weeks old. They join their mother on hunting trips at 3 to 4 months old and can kill their own prey by the age of two years.

DIET Lions eat anything they can catch and kill: wildebeest, impala and other antelopes, buffalo, giraffe, hogs and zebra. They also feed on smaller animals like hares, insects and birds.

PREDATORS In the first few years, cubs are vulnerable to attack from cheetahs, leopards, jackals and hyenas. Adult lions have almost no predators except for buffalo and rhino when provoked. Humans are their main threat and loss of habitat.

FAMILY Male lions protect their pride, or family unit, by patrolling an area covering about 260 kilometres. They mark bushes with urine so other lions won't come into their territory.

LIFE SPAN From 10 to 15 years in the wild and up to 25 years in captivity.

NUMBERS REMAINING
An estimated 23,000 lions remain in Africa. Around 300 Asiatic lions are protected in the Gir National Park, South West India. There are 200 white lions kept in captivity around the world.

CREATING LENA THE LION BOOK

A lion kill just a metre from my jeep.

Two of the young lions I walked with in Zambia.

My tent at Rekero camp in the the Maasi Mara.

“The first time a huge male lion walked past my jeep, just a metre away, I was breathless with fear. When I realised he wasn’t going to jump into the jeep, I relaxed and spent many hours taking photographs and writing about the lion’s behaviour.

I love watching lion cubs. They are so entertaining. They’re always getting into mischief, biting mum’s tail and annoying dad. When a kill is made, each lion fights for its share and the sound of their roaring is deafening.

One morning in the Maasi Mara, I had a huge lion close to my tent. He was calling his three sons who were on the other side of the river, and my tent was in the middle. It was exciting and terrifying.

I had an amazing once-in-a-lifetime experience in Zambia. I walked with four young lions for an hour in the bush with three guides! One guide gave me a sturdy stick and said if a lion misbehaved I should point the stick at it and shout a very loud ***no!*** Thankfully, I didn’t have to do that.”

Jan Latta, author and wildlife photographer.

QUESTIONS

1. Where do lions live?
2. What is a pride of lions?
3. What is a pug mark?
4. What time of the day do lions hunt?
5. What do lions eat?
6. What is a carnivore?
7. Are white lions albinos?
8. Can lions swim?
9. Can lion cubs see when they are born?
10. What is the lifespan of lions in the wild?

MAKE A LION'S FACE
Fill in the left side of the lion's face using the right side as a guide. Print it, cut it out and wear it as a mask. Grrr!

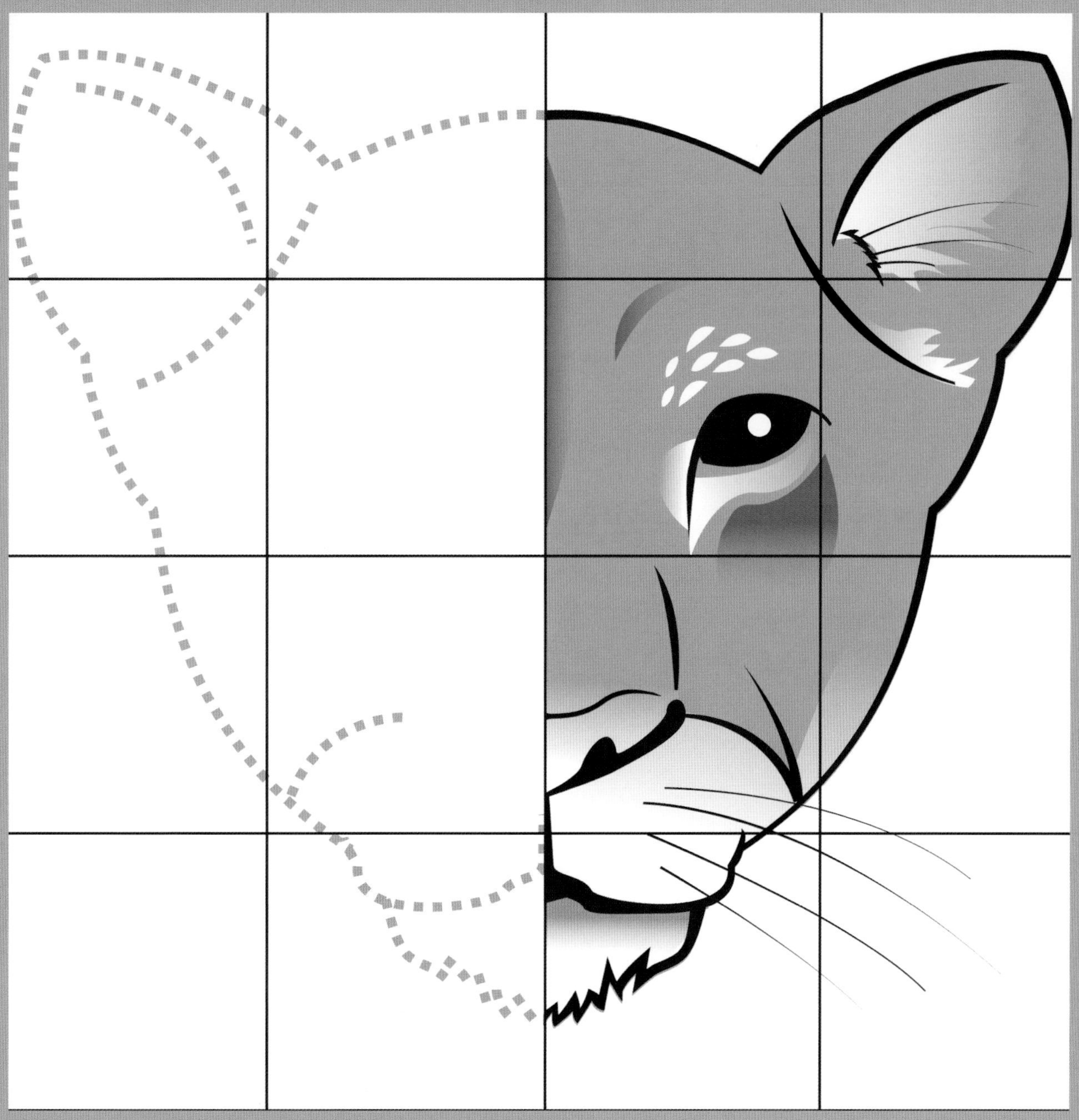

THOMAS HAMLYN-HARRIS

Have some fun creating and wearing animal masks!

On white felt, or heavy paper, draw the panda's eyes, nose and mouth. Glue on ears. Cut out holes for your eyes to see. Add black socks on your hands for paws. Then you can be a panda in a bamboo forest in China.

Cut out an oval shape on cardboard and paint a sloth's face on it. Make holes for your eyes to see. Put on your mask, and move very, very, slowly, just like a sloth.

ORANGUTAN ORANGES

Make an orangutan face on an orange. Stick on sultanas for eyes and nose and draw on a smile. Use strips of orange paper for its long hair.

PAPER PAWS

Draw the shape of a leopard's paw on two paper bags and paint them yellow. Add big black leopard spots and claws with a black marker. Wear your fierce leopard paws!

Draw a **LEOPON** a cross between a female lioness and a male leopard. Have lots of fun with your imagination.

MEERKAT FINGER PUPPETS

Place two pieces of paper flat in front of you and put your forefinger on top. Draw around the outline of your finger and cut out the shape allowing at least a centimetre extra space. Staple the top and sides together keeping the bottom edges open. Draw the face, arms legs and add a tail.

CHEETAH WORD GAME

- How many words can you make out of the word cheetah?
- You should be able to make at least five words.
- Have fun looking at the letters. Try putting them in different sequences to find new words.

Paint large and small paper plates grey. Glue on ears and a black nose. Draw a smiley mouth and make holes for your eyes to see. Pick gum leaves and branches and pretend to be a koala in the trees.

ANIMAL SUPERSTARS

Look for TV advertisements featuring wild animals. Why do you think that animal has been used for the ad.

GIRAFFE DOT DRAWING

Draw the outline of a giraffe on paper. Make a dot painting with brown, orange and yellow paints for its coat. Add the face, hooves and mane in black.

GUMLEAF PRINT

Collect gum leaves and make a paper rubbing of the leaves. Place a flattened leaf under a piece of paper and gently rub a crayon over the top, making sure you don't move the paper.

RHINO RESCUE

- Make a list of all the endangered rhinos in the world.
- How many are close to being extinct?
- How many have disappeared from earth?
- How many are critically endangered?
- What is happening to save them?

ZIPPY ZEBRAS

Make a zebra face with a cone of white paper, then paint on the black stripes, eyes, black nose and stick-on ears. Attach to a long stick, add strips of black paper for the giraffe's mane and gallop around making zebra noises.

ANIMAL ANCESTORS

Research the names of animals that were alive during the Ice Age. A woolly ancestor of the elephant roamed the earth. What was its name? Draw its picture. Why did it become extinct?

CHIMP CHOPSTICKS

Head outdoors, crouch down and use a wooden chopstick as a chimp's tool to forage for food in the ground. Record what you see at chimp level.

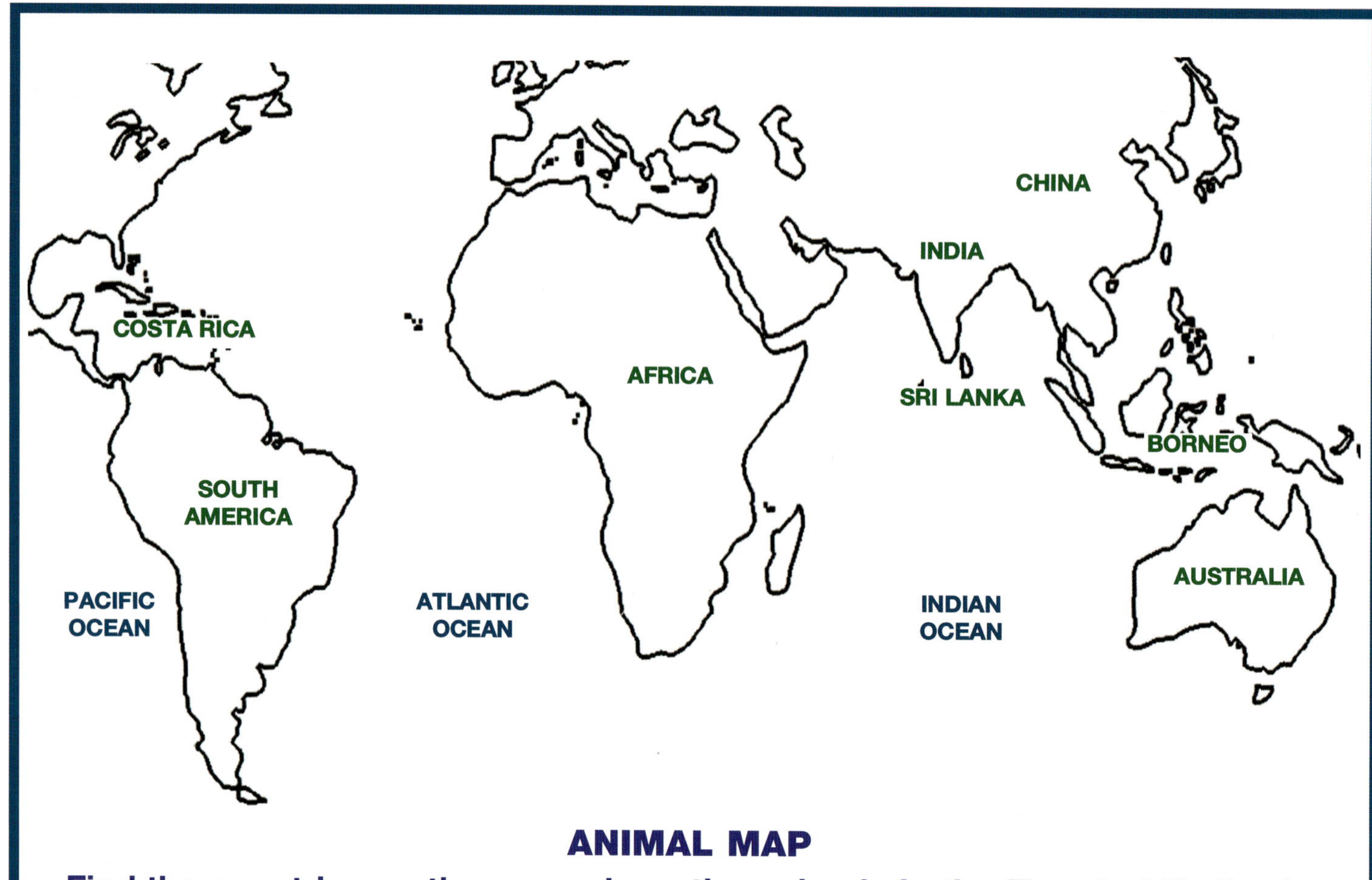

ANIMAL MAP

Find the countries on the map where the animals in the *True to Life Books* live in the wild. Add the animals and their habitats.

COLLECTIVE QUIZ

Some groups of animals are described using collective nouns. Here are some from the *True to Life Books*:

A journey of giraffes
A herd of elephants
A pod of hippos
A pride of lions
A crash of rhinos
A leap of leopards
A swift of tigers
A litter of cubs

How many collective nouns can you add for animals?

DIARY OF A SAFARI

Write about your exciting safari adventures in Africa! Watch the animal videos **www.truetolifebooks.com.au** to inspire your creativity.

What animals might you see?
Where will you stop to camp?
Do you live in a tent?
Describe your guide.
What dangers might you face?
Will you see animals hunting?
How will you travel between camps?
What foods will you eat?
Will you be frightened at night?

colour in the lion family

SERENA GEDDES

DID YOU KNOW?

- Lions were drawn in cave paintings 15,000 years ago.
- They are the second biggest in the cat family, after the tiger.
- They are the only big cats to form social groups.
- Female lions hunt more than 90% of the time, compared with males.
- Lions are not good hunters. Only 20% to 30% of their attempts are successful.
- The leading cause of cub death is starvation because cubs are always the last to feed at a kill.

INTERESTING WEBSITES

AFRICAN WILDLIFE FOUNDATION
www.awf.org

THE CAT SURVIVAL TRUST
www.catsurvivaltrust.org

LION ADOPTIONS
www.adoption.co.uk/lion/

WORLD WIDE FUND FOR NATURE
www.panda.org

NATIONAL GEOGRAPHIC
www.nationalgeographic.com

KIDS' PLANET www.kidsplanet.org

SCIENCE KIDS
www.sciencekids.co.nz/science-facts/animals/lion.html

See Lena the Lion video and exciting videos of wild animals from the True to Life Books *www.truetolifebooks.com.au*